Storyline Wildlife

Book 3

Harry Stanton and Audrey Daly

Oliver & Boyd

Acknowledgements

The authors and publishers wish to thank the following for permission to reproduce the photographs listed: Ardea London 9 (bottom), 48, 60 (both), 61 (all), 65 (all), 81, 84; Sdeuard C Bisserot 93 (both), 96 (both); Biofotos 49; Sidney J Clarke 41 (top), 44 (left), 45 (top right); Bruce Coleman Ltd cover; Ron and Christine Foord 85 (all), 88 (all); Forestry Commission 34, 35, 38; David Henrie, Edinburgh 8 (bottom left), 29 (bottom right), 36–7, 40 (both), 41 (middle), 45 (top left, bottom left, bottom right), 53 (insert); Natural Image 25 (top both, bottom left), 32, 33 (all), 53 (top), 68, 69 (all), 72; NHPA 9 (top), 15, 17 (both), 24, 52, 64, 73, 76, 77 (left all, bottom right); Oxford Scientific Films 25 (bottom right), 77 (top right), 89; Popperfoto 19; Harry Stanton 8 (top, bottom right), 12, 13 (both), 21, 28 (both), 29 (top, bottom right), 41 (bottom), 44 (left), 53 (bottom), 80; James Young 56.

Thanks are due also to John Marshall for producing the illustrations on pages 54, 59, and 74.

Oliver & Boyd
Robert Stevenson House
1–3 Baxter's Place
Leith Walk
Edinburgh EH1 3BB

A Division of Longman Group UK Ltd

ISBN 0 05 003814 1
First published 1986
© Harry Stanton and Audrey Daly 1986

All rights reserved; no part of this publication may be reproduced, stored in a retrieval system, or transmitted in any form or by any means, electronic, mechanical, photocopying, recording or otherwise, without the prior written permission of the Publishers.

Set in 12/18pt Monophoto Plantin
Produced by Longman Group (FE) Limited
Printed in Hong Kong

Contents

Willoughby's Story   page 4
Zoos   13
Crocodiles and Alligators   15
Cuckoo Pint   28
Bluebells   29
Norway Spruce   31
Ash Trees   33
Building New Forests   34
Nothing But Trees   36
One Fungus + One Fungus = Two Fungi   41
Donna's Day Out   47
Horses   53
The Great Spotted Woodpecker   56
Parrots   58
Snakes   67
The End of a Perfect Day   80
Insects   85
Bats   91

Willoughby's Story

Willoughby sat thinking. He really didn't like writing stories. He never seemed to get good ideas, somehow. His twin sister Donna was much better at it than he was. On the other side of the room, her black face was thoughtful as she started to write.

Slowly Willoughby got his brain to work. What was he supposed to be writing about, anyhow? Conservation? Now, what did that mean? It was so hot in the classroom that he was nearly falling asleep. Oh yes, it meant trying to stop super animals like elephants and tigers – and even little animals like the red squirrel he sometimes saw in the woods – from dying out altogether.

He frowned. That wouldn't be a good idea at all.

Red squirrel

Fancy only having pictures of them! Well, he could say that to start with. He wrote it down and went on thinking.

Hadn't he seen something about bears lately? Then he remembered. There had been a television programme about them, and some things had been said about conservation, because some bears are quite rare nowadays.

There are seven kinds of bears, and all except one (the spectacled bear of South America) live in the northern half or hemisphere of the world. People used to think that there were as many as two hundred different kinds of bears, because some kinds come in more than one colour.

The most widespread of all bears, the brown bear, varies in size and colour depending on where it lives. Brown bears aren't even all brown. They can be nearly black and they can be a pale yellowish colour. Grizzly bears in North America are brown bears as well, but their fur is brown tipped with grey. The largest flesh-eating animal on land is a brown bear – the Kodiak bear – which can be as tall as 3 metres and weigh 780 kilograms. It lives in the northernmost parts of the United States, in Alaska. The American black bear can be almost any colour as well – chocolate, tan, grey and even white.

All bears are usually shaggy-haired and solidly built. Most animals, like cats and dogs, walk on their toes, but bears walk like people, on the soles of their feet.

Bears will eat both animal and vegetable foods, and they enjoy sweet things like honey. (Because of this, they are the only animals which get cavities in their teeth.)

They are among the most dangerous animals in the world, for several reasons. They have very sharp claws and teeth, they have uncertain tempers, and they are enormously strong. The brown bear of Europe is so strong that it can kill a cow with one blow from its paw, and the grizzly bear of North America could kill a 500-kilogram bison with its huge forepaws.

Willoughby remembered the polar bears which he had seen swimming at London Zoo. He liked them nearly as much as elephants and tigers, and he thought they were great. Not long ago they were an endangered species, but now their numbers are increasing because they are internationally protected. They are completely protected in Russia, which is thought to have the largest polar bear colony in the world, on the Arctic islands of Wrangel and Herald. "I'll mention that," thought Willoughby, writing it down. "After all, that's conservation."

He had read once about polar bears in America being hunted from helicopters, so that they could never escape. People are the only animals that hunt other animals just for sport, he thought. A lot of animals are dying off because they've been hunted so much. There's the Asian lion – there are fewer than two hundred left in the whole of Asia because of people hunting them. And how about the Arabian oryx – hunted from fast cars by the Arabs, and with no way of getting away. They're protected now, but are there enough of them left to breed and survive?

Suddenly Willoughby remembered throwing stones at frogs when he was a very small boy. He had been enjoying himself until his mother had caught him. "A long time ago," she had said gently, "a famous man from Greece said, 'Boys throw stones at frogs for fun, but the frogs die in earnest.'" And they had looked down together at two small dead frogs.

"I'm no better than those hunters," thought Willoughby, his black face growing even darker with shame. "But I've never done anything like that since. Anyway, no one should hunt animals for fun, just as trophies to hang on the wall, or soon there won't be any left alive at all." He remembered that he was supposed to be writing a story, so he wrote that thought down too.

On pages 8 and 9 there are
some pictures of rare animals.
The story continues on page 10.

Polar bears are now protected by law.

The American black bear has shorter fur, shorter claws and shorter hind feet than the brown bear.

The brown bear varies in size and colour depending on where it lives.

The Arabian oryx is a very rare animal.

The white-throated wallaby now lives only in New Zealand.

He went back to the bears again. At one time brown bears could be found all over Europe, but now they are found only in small pockets here and there, because they've been hunted so much. "There's more to it than that, though," thought Willoughby. "They live in mountain areas and coniferous forests nowadays, instead of the deciduous forests where they used to live.

"It's people again," Willoughby said to himself. "They cut down the forests to make room for farms to grow crops, destroying the bears' habitat, so that the bears had to find new places to live. That's what happened to that white-throated wallaby that Donna likes so much. Its habitat was destroyed in Australia, and it is extinct there now. It only lives in New Zealand. But the wallaby's habitat was destroyed because people brought things like rabbits to Australia, and the native animals suffered because the new animals ate the food that they needed.

"That's two more things we shouldn't do." Willoughby wrote them down – destroying habitats, and bringing in new kinds of animals that don't belong.

"It's all people," he thought. "Even when they think they're being clever and catching animals to put in zoos so that they can breed and the species will be all right, they're often doing the wrong thing, like with the orang-utans of Borneo and Sumatra." For every young animal that is captured and actually reaches a zoo, several others die on the way, usually including the mother of the young orang-utan.

People are dangerous to animals in other ways – and to themselves as well indirectly.

Oil pollution kills birds and fish – and the detergents used to clean up the oil often don't help.

Insecticides like DDT that are used to kill insects that eat or destroy crops can be dangerous to animals many kilometres from where they are used. That's because some of the insecticide finds its way into streams and rivers and so down to the sea. Research has shown that some of the fish from the Baltic Sea can be poisonous to people if they eat them regularly – because the Baltic Sea is so polluted by DDT!

The bell rang for home time just as Willoughby finished his story. He looked through the pages for a moment – had he really written all that? Then he handed the sheets to Mrs Evans on the way out. Next moment, kicking a football with his friends, he'd forgotten all about it.

It was nearly a month later before he remembered it again. He had won a prize from the County Council for the best written work on conservation!

11

When they heard what the prize was, the whole class cheered. They were all going to the zoo for the day!

Willoughby himself was delighted – but he was also a bit puzzled. He knew he wasn't at all good at writing stories.

Zoos

This gorilla lives in a town zoo.

About 3000 years ago, King Solomon of Israel kept wild animals in a zoo. Around the same time, a ruler in China also kept a zoo. His name was Wen Wang, and he called his zoo the "Garden of Intelligence".

That was about a thousand years before Jesus was born. Nearer our own time, the ancient Greeks kept animals in zoos. So did the ancient Romans. A Roman emperor called Octavius Augustus had an enormous zoo. It had 420 tigers in it, and 260 lions, as well as hundreds of other animals.

In those days, zoos were simply collections of wild animals for people to look at. Nowadays, a zoo is much more than that. In a modern zoo, people can study the animals and learn all sorts of things about them.

There is another reason why zoos are very important. Have you ever heard of the Red Data Book? It has lists in it of all kinds of animals that are in danger of becoming extinct. That means that if nothing is done about the animals in those lists, there will be none left alive anywhere in the whole world. They are called endangered species, and the Red Data Book gives

These bison live in a safari park.

the number of each kind that are left in the world. Tigers and elephants are included amongst many others.

So one of the main reasons why zoos are important is that they help to save endangered species, and try to breed them in captivity.

Amongst the animals that have been saved by zoos are the wisent (European bison), and a strange deer from China called Père David's Deer. If zoos hadn't taken care of some of these, there would be none left at all.

More and more baby animals are being born in zoos these days. One day zoos may have enough animals to be able to send some back into the wild to live, instead of capturing them to put them in cages.

There are many different kinds of zoos. Some zoos have a mixed collection of animals and birds and reptiles. Zoos in towns are often like this, with cages for the animals, sometimes with an outdoor enclosure added.

Some animals are only awake at night (they are called nocturnal animals). They are often kept in buildings lit by a dim light or a red light. Their normal way of life is changed so that they can be seen moving about when the zoo is open in daylight hours.

Some people think that it is cruel to keep animals in cages. But a modern zoo isn't a prison for the animals. They are usually kept with their own kind – in pairs or in herds.

Even in the wild, most animals can't really be said to be free, in the way people are. Each one has to keep to its own little piece of the world – and often fight for it too.

In any case, not all zoos keep animals in cages. There are safari parks which you drive through in a car. The animals there seem to be almost completely free. Baboons will climb on to the car, and giraffes will look down at you with their gentle eyes. And in open range zoos, the animals are given as much space and freedom as possible.

Zoos cost much more to run today than at any time in the past. They need a great many people to look after them, as well. In spite of this, there are more and more zoos. There are now over a thousand in the world!

Crocodiles and Alligators

All the members of the crocodilian family are reptiles with tough, armoured skins. They are amphibians, living in and beside lakes and rivers, and even the sea in the warmer parts of the world.

The Romans were probably the first Europeans to see a reptile of this kind. They gave it the name "crocodile" when their armies invaded North Africa.

We sometimes call them "living fossils", because they are very closely related to the dinosaurs which died out a hundred and fifty million years ago. At the time of the dinosaurs, the largest crocodile was over 15 metres long!

The largest one known to people more recently was killed in the Philippine Islands in 1823. It weighed about 2 tonnes, and was over 8 metres long from the tip of its nose to the end of its tail.

Estuarine crocodile

Present-day crocodiles aren't as big as that. Estuarine crocodiles, which live in salt water along the coasts and estuaries of Asia and Australia, are the biggest. They can grow to over 6 metres long. They are also the only ones which are known to swim out to sea.

When crocodiles are mentioned, most people think of the Nile crocodile. It lives in parts of Africa and in Madagascar, and is sometimes hunted because of its attacks on cattle. There are however about 23 species of crocodilians left in the world – we know of over a hundred extinct species. They fall into three main groups: crocodiles; alligators; and their smaller cousins the caimans, and gavials.

Alligators live in the south-east of the United States and in China. Caimans live in the rivers of South America, and gavials live in southern Asia. You can tell an alligator from a crocodile because the fourth tooth on a crocodile's lower jaw can be seen when its mouth is shut. A crocodile also has a slightly narrower snout than an alligator. Gavials have long very narrow snouts and live mainly on fish.

When you look closely at a photograph of a crocodile, you may see a little bird sitting quite fearlessly on its head or even in its mouth. Such birds pick off the insects living on the crocodile's

Adult Nile crocodile showing its lethal teeth

Baby Nile crocodile hatching

back, and they clean its teeth, feeding on the scraps of food left in its mouth. They are called crocodile birds.

All crocodilians have sharp pointed teeth. When a tooth gets worn out or damaged, a new one takes its place. A crocodile's teeth may be replaced as many as thirty or forty times in the creature's life.

In spite of their sharp teeth, however, crocodilians cannot chew. So they have to swallow large pieces of food whole. They also swallow large stones which help to grind up the food in their stomachs.

Baby crocodiles feed on insects and small fish. Then as they grow larger, they eat frogs, small animals, larger fish and even crocodiles smaller than themselves. They will also capture water birds. Only the biggest crocodiles will lie in wait for large animals such as buffaloes, antelopes and sometimes elephants.

Eyes, ears and nostrils are all on the top of a crocodilian's head. This is so that it can watch, listen and breathe while the rest of its body is underwater. With only the top of its head showing it can move quietly, without making the smallest ripple, towards its prey, until it is close enough to grab it. Then the unfortunate victim has little chance of escape.

Crocodiles, like all the other members of the crocodilian family, spend most of their lives keeping their bodies at the right temperature. At night when the land grows colder, they hunt for food in the water. During the day, they climb out and lie basking in the sunshine. Unlike humans, they cannot sweat, so they open their huge mouths to let the moisture in their mouths evaporate to make them cooler. When they become so hot that this doesn't help any more, they slip back into the water to cool down.

Both alligators and crocodiles dig burrows in the banks of rivers, so that they can shelter in very cold or very hot weather. They always make their burrows big enough to give themselves room to turn round. This is so that they can look out to see if another animal is approaching.

Eyes, ears and nostrils are all on the top of a crocodile's head.

Not many reptiles have the kind of voice that crocodilians have. Both males and females can bellow very loudly.

All crocodilians lay eggs. Some lay as many as ninety, each about the size of a very large hen's egg. They are laid in a hole about half a metre deep, then covered with sand. The sun's warmth helps to hatch them out.

Alligators lay their eggs in a nest of mud and vegetation. As the vegetation rots, it gives out heat, which helps to hatch out the eggs in the same way as the sun's heat helps with the eggs of other crocodilians. The female guards the nest until the young hatch out. If she did not do this, other animals would eat the eggs.

It can take between six and fourteen weeks for the eggs to hatch, depending on the kind of crocodilian. Each baby has a sharp spike on the end of its snout with which it breaks through the shell. (Adults are never seen with these spikes, because they drop off soon after hatching.)

As soon as they have hatched, the young crocodilians begin to squeak, and the mother digs them out of the nest. Otherwise they would not be able to get out. The mother takes her young ones to the water and guards them. Although she looks after them for several weeks, most of the babies will be eaten by other animals and birds, and few will grow into adults.

People are the most dangerous enemies that crocodilians have in the wild, because they use the hide for fine handbags and luggage. Probably few crocodilians live longer than thirty years in the wild, for they have many other enemies as well.

They are however long-lived as a species. Some crocodilians have been known to live over fifty years in captivity.

How do you know this is an alligator not a crocodile?

Octopuses

The octopus must surely be one of the strangest of all the strange creatures in the world. It has eight long arms or tentacles round its head, and it is from these it gets its name, because *octo* is the Latin word for eight. Each tentacle has two rows of suckers along its length. The tentacles of the common octopus are less than a metre long, but those of the largest octopuses – octopus apollyon which lives off the western coast of the United States – have tentacles as long as 4.5 metres.

Octopuses live in nearly every sea in the world, although there aren't many in the polar seas of the Arctic and Antarctic. They live on the bottom of the sea, on sand or on rocky reefs, squeezing their soft rubbery bodies into small holes in the rocks. Sometimes they even live in little "towns", each animal marking its own territory with a stone or some shells.

The eyes of an octopus look just like human eyes, and they work in the same way. It has a horny beak which looks like a parrot's beak. Sometimes it uses its arms to move slowly around the seabed. It has a strange funnel however which squirts out a water jet to propel the octopus along when it wants to swim. This funnel is also used to squirt out a stream of black ink in the face of enemies such as big fish, when the octopus is trying to escape. Another way an octopus can defend itself is by changing colour to merge with its surroundings.

Octopuses are more intelligent than most sea creatures. They show a great deal of cunning when hunting. They can stalk their prey very patiently, and will even wriggle the tips of their arms to make them look like worms to attract small fish. They live on fish, lobsters, mussels and crabs, which they kill by a special poison produced by their salivary glands. Only one octopus – the spotted octopus which lives in the Indian Ocean – can poison people.

An octopus egg looks like a grain of rice. The eggs are laid in strings and fastened under rocky overhangs. The female octopus looks after the eggs until they hatch, and sometimes dies of starvation afterwards.

One of the most surprising things about the octopus is the family it belongs to – the molluscs – and the other animals it is related to. The word mollusc means "soft-bodied", and all molluscs have soft bodies. They have no bones and no proper skeleton. Some molluscs, like garden snails and

There are some pictures of molluscs on pages 24 and 25. The story continues on page 26.

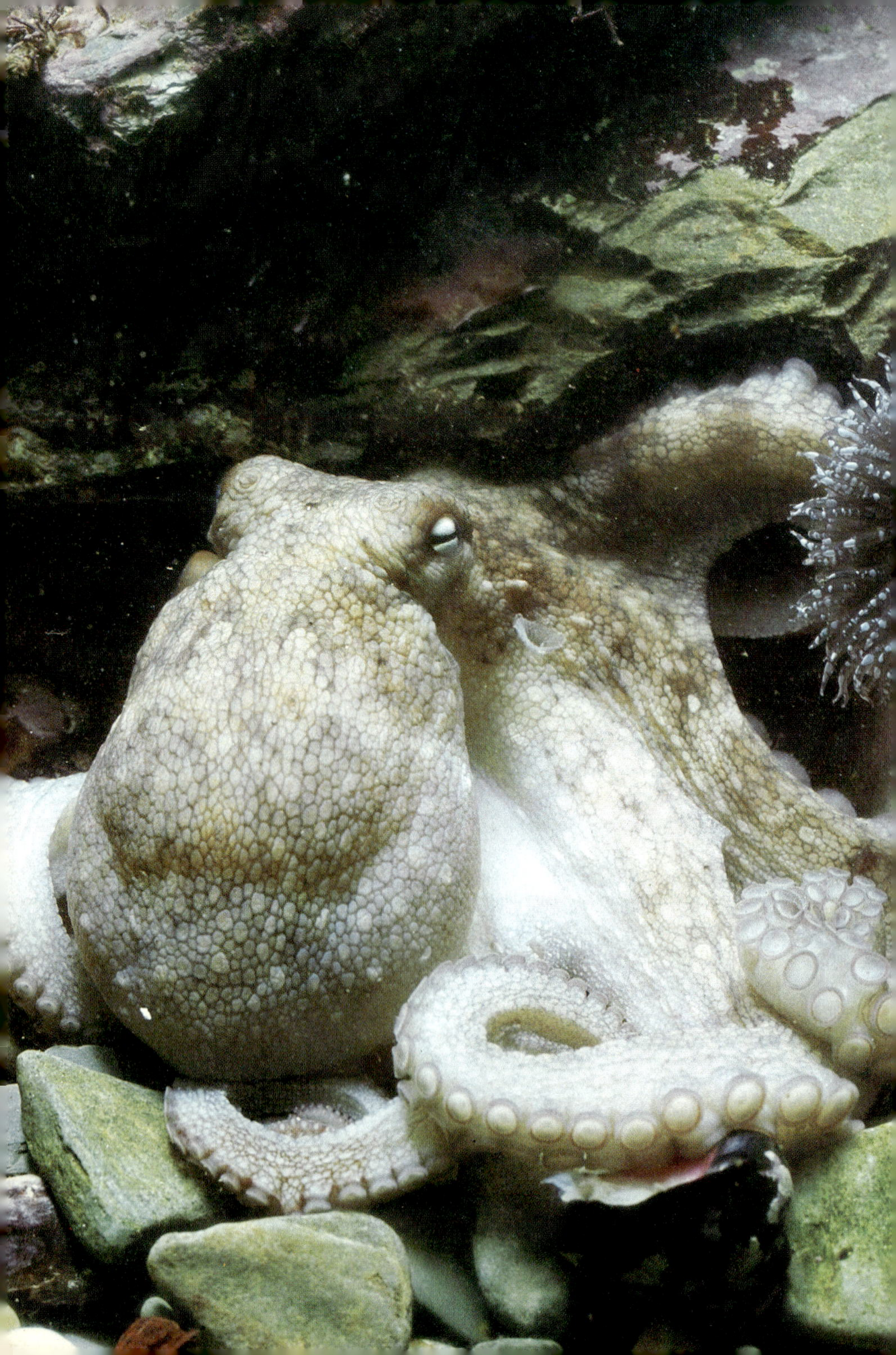

Mating garden snails

Eggs of a garden snail

Adult garden snails with young

Fossil of an extinct mollusc

25

oysters and mussels, have a hard shell to protect them. Some, such as squids and cuttlefish, have a thin shell inside their bodies to strengthen them. Octopuses and the fat slugs you see in the garden are also molluscs, but have no shell at all.

Molluscs are found all over the world, in every kind of place where animals live. We know that there were molluscs in the very earliest ages of the Earth – about six hundred million years ago – because of the fossils which have been found.

The biggest molluscs are the giant squids, close cousins of the octopus. The largest ever measured – in 1878 in Canada – was nearly 17 metres long, its tentacles being over 10 metres!

Squids have ten tentacles altogether, and are jet-propelled when they swim, in the same way as octopuses, although they are much faster. Some deep-sea squids carry their own light with them in the ocean darkness. They have special light organs which are thought to be for attracting prey.

The most familiar mollusc to many people is the snail. There are 120 species of snail living in Britain. Eighty of them live on land, and the others in fresh water.

The snail's body is all in one, from the foot on which it moves along so slowly to the head with its two pairs of tentacles. One pair has eyes at the tips. (Snails which live in fresh water have only one pair of tentacles, with eyes at the base.) The snail's "home" is a whorled shell made mainly of chalk. It usually has a right-handed spiral, but the ram's horn snail is an exception, being left-handed.

Land snails eat plants and fruit, mosses and fungi. Garden snails will even eat dead slugs and worms. Snails that live in fresh water usually eat algae. The great pond snail however will also eat small newts, dead beetle larvae, and sometimes sticklebacks.

The biggest snail in the world is the African giant snail, and the largest one ever measured was 39.3 centimetres from snout to tail. It weighed 900 grams! The biggest one found in Britain is the Roman snail which can be about 10 centimetres long and weigh 85 grams.

In spite of the stories about "snail pace", snails don't move quite as slowly as you might think. The common garden snail has been clocked at 50.3 metres an hour!

Cuckoo Pint

Cuckoo pint, Lords and Ladies, parson in the pulpit, Adam and Eve, Wake Robin and wild arum are all names for one of the strangest plants to be seen in the countryside.

The cuckoo pint likes shade, and appears under hedges and in woodlands in April. The plant has a cowl-like green and purple sheath wrapped round a club-shaped spike. Hidden below the spike are tiny flowers without petals. When small flies and insects visit the flowers, they can't escape because of downward-pointing hairs that keep them inside the sheath.

Long ago, in the time of the first Queen Elizabeth, the roots of the cuckoo pint plant were used to make starch to stiffen the enormous ruffs (collars) that were worn in those days.

The cuckoo pint likes shady places.

The berries are poisonous – do not pick them!

Bluebells

Because they can grow in the shade, bluebells are found in the woods *after* the trees have grown their canopy of leaves. The lovely blue-purple bell-shaped flowers often cover the ground completely, making it look like a blue carpet gently swaying in the wind.

Bluebells

Harebells

Each plant starts from a roundish bulb about 25 millimetres in diameter, beneath the ground. When the leaves grow in spring, they lie close to the earth, and they may grow as long as 30 centimetres before the even longer flower stalk appears.

Five or six flowers hang on each plant, filling the woods with the most delightful scent in April, May and June.

There are several other names for bluebells in England. They may be called blue bonnets, wood bells, and pride of the wood. In Scotland, these same flowers are called wild hyacinths.

The plants known as bluebells of Scotland are called harebells or windbells in England. These delicate plants are found on heathland, hilly pasture land, and along roadsides. Their lower leaves are heart-shaped with long stalks, but by the time the flowers are seen, the leaves have disappeared!

In Ireland, the bluebells of Scotland are known as fairy bells, or goblins' thimbles.

Norway Spruce

Most people know just what a Norway spruce looks like – because it's the tree we call a Christmas tree. When it is fully grown, it can reach heights of over 50 metres. These trees have very shallow roots, however, so that they can easily be uprooted by strong winds.

Although coniferous trees of this kind have been known to live as long as six hundred years, their lifespan is usually about a hundred and fifty years. The Norway spruce grows in Britain and all over Europe. It is used a great deal in reforestation both here and in North America.

Its bark is dark brown, thin and scaly, and it has dark green leaves which are 1 millimetre wide and nearly 25 millimetres long. Looked at end-on, they are squarish in shape, and they stay on the tree for several years – sometimes as long as seven years.

The Norway spruce has two kinds of flowers. In May it has yellow catkins which are male flowers, and the wind takes pollen from these to the small pink candles which are female flowers.

The pink candles later change into brown cones. These cones contain seeds which are released on warm windy days in the following spring.

Young Norway spruce cones developing

The wood of the spruce is known as white wood or white deal, and is very tough. When telegraph poles or planks are needed, each is cut in one piece from a large tree.

Most newspapers and magazines are made from wood pulp which is made from young Norway spruce trees.

Ash Trees

The ash tree is so graceful that it is sometimes known as the "Venus of the woods". It is easy to recognise in winter, because it has black buds at the ends of its twigs, from autumn right through to spring.

In spring, the flowers appear first. They grow in loose clusters at the ends of twigs, and they are easily missed because they are small and green in colour.

The beautiful leaves appear much later than those of any other tree. Each leaf has a long thin stalk with three or more pairs of leaflets growing on it, and there is always a single leaflet at the end of the stalk.

When the flowers become seeds, they hang in large bunches called ash keys or spinners. Each separate seed has a little twisted wing which causes it to spin as it falls to the ground, seed end first.

The wood of the ash is very strong.

Winter bud of ash

Ash keys

Building New Forests

Forestry worker in Wales felling a tree

Hundreds of years ago, more than a third of Britain was covered in trees.

By the time Queen Victoria came to the throne in 1837, many of those trees had gone. They had been chopped down to make way for farms, and for use in industry. No new trees had ever been planted to take their place. Only one-twentieth of Britain now had trees on it.

The land was poorer in many ways. There was much less wildlife, and the landscape was harsher. High ground could not be farmed without trees to give shelter to animals and crops. Timber that was needed had to be bought from other countries. Even things like walking and nature study weren't so interesting without trees.

Something had to be done!

So at last, in 1919, the Forestry Commission was formed. It began by planting conifers in many parts of Britain.

Now when trees are felled, new trees take their place. Whole new forests are growing on heaths and moors and hillsides that are no good for farming.

Slowly the amount of land with trees on it has been creeping up. Today it is almost one-twelfth of the whole country, and there is hope for Britain's forests.

This area has been restocked with sitka spruce and Japanese larch.

Nothing But Trees

The wind had turned cold. In the little car park in the forest, people were packing up. Picnic cups and plates were put away, and rugs were folded. Time to go home!

One car drove off, then another. An Asian mother clicked her seat belt into place, then looked round at the children in the back seat. "Where's Aruna?" she asked.

"I think she went in the other car with Uncle Ram," said her young son.

Aerial view of a coniferous forest

"Well, she's not here, and they've gone," said Mrs Patel. "I suppose she must be with them. There's no one else left in the car park." As she drove off, she went on, "This is a really good place for a picnic. We'll come here again. The foresters and other people in the Forestry Commission seem to do much more than just look after trees!"

There were no cars left. The wind dropped, and the forest grew still. Now a different sound could be heard. Someone was crying. From time to time, a little voice called, "Mummy, Mummy, where are you?" Then silence fell again.

Further up the track from the car park, near the top of the hill, a forester was working. He would have agreed with Mrs Patel – he certainly did do much more than just look after trees. He planted new trees when old trees were chopped down. He protected birds and other wildlife, and tried to make the forest interesting for people to visit.

Last month he and another forester had made a Nature Trail for people to follow. He'd helped to make the car park and the campsite – and the track so that people could drive into the forest. And he always had to watch in case fires started.

At the moment he was weeding the ground between some small trees that had been planted to take the place of some burned down in a fire. He wanted to get the row done before dark.

He worked steadily until there was hardly any light left. Then he stood up and went thankfully back to his van beside the track. He paused for a moment, enjoying the quiet evening. Then he climbed in, and drove down the bumpy track.

As he drove past the car park, his lights picked up several bits of paper lying around. He got out of his van and picked them up. When he opened the litter bin to drop them in, the little voice started to cry once more.

"Where are you?" he shouted. "Keep calling, and I'll come and find you."

Five minutes later he was lifting the little Asian girl into his van to take her home. She could hardly speak for sobbing as he tried to find out where she lived. "It was just trees," she said, over and over again. "Nothing but trees."

Luckily Mrs Patel had discovered that her daughter was missing, and she drove into the car park at that moment. She told the forester how the mistake had happened.

He smiled as he looked down at Aruna. "Never mind, all's well that ends well," he said. "Just don't get lost in my forest again!"

Many forests now have special areas like this where people can sit and have a picnic under the trees.

In forests there is always a risk of fire, especially in hot, dry weather. Special beaters for putting out fires are kept beside warning notices all through the forest.

One Fungus + One Fungus = Two Fungi

No matter where you look, you will find fungi. Fungi are everywhere. They are in the air. They are in the soil. They are in the water of lakes, rivers and seas. They are on and inside animals and plants, in food, in people's clothes, and in the human body.

Fly agaric is very poisonous.

Chanterelle

Amanita – a type of cap fungus

This family of plants is strange in more ways than just its name. Fungi are so different from other plants that many scientists do not think that they are plants at all. Fungi have no roots, stems, leaves or flowers, and one fungus can look completely different from another. Both the mildew that forms on stale food and the mushrooms that we can see growing are fungi. The family includes yeasts, moulds, mildews and mushrooms, and it is important to people in both good and bad ways.

In 1928, a scientist called Alexander Fleming found some green mould growing on a dish which had bacteria in it. The mould had killed the bacteria – and the world's first and most famous antibiotic, penicillin, was discovered because Alexander Fleming saw what had happened. Penicillin has cured infections in countless numbers of people.

Yeast is a fungus which we use to make bread light and soft, and the blue in blue cheeses such as Stilton and Danish Blue is caused by fungi. We eat mushrooms and truffles – they are both fungi, and so is the alcohol in beer and wine.

On the other hand, the diseases ringworm and athlete's foot are both caused by fungi. Mould on food can be very dangerous. Mildew on plants can ruin a crop. In the Middle Ages, about five hundred years ago, a kind of mildew called ergot grew on the rye which was ground into flour for bread. It caused madness and many deaths when people ate the infected bread. Even today great care has to be taken in the storage of food, because not only can fungus ruin the food but thousands of people might be poisoned.

Fungi can kill trees – Dutch elm disease is caused by a fungus.

Those members of the fungus family which we can easily see, like the mushrooms we eat, and toadstools found growing on a log of wood, can't grow in soil. Instead, they take their nourishment from living and dead plants.

Each fungus is very simple, made up of fine branching threads called hyphae. Even the cap of a large mushroom is made up of these tiny threads, all matted together.

Fungi do not have seeds. They reproduce themselves from spores. A spore is a tiny cell that is so light that it can be carried by a breeze to any part of the Earth's surface. But the spore will only develop into a fungus if it lands upon a damp surface where it can grow.

In toadstools and mushrooms, the caps are the parts which produce the spores. A field mushroom can produce forty million spores in an hour, so it is not surprising that they are always present in the air. Most large fungi have a stalk and a cap, like the edible mushroom. The beautiful and poisonous fly agaric has a reddish cap and a firm stalk, but a large number of fungi such as the bracket fungus which grows on the trunks of trees, and the giant puffball, have no stalks.

Fungi can be very different in both size and colour. There are toadstools complete with stalk and cap which only measure a few millimetres in height. They live on rotting wood and dead leaves. There are also huge fungi like the giant puffball. The largest of these ever discovered was found in Derbyshire and was over one and a half metres in diameter. The largest fungus ever found growing on a tree weighed about 140 kilograms and was 142 centimetres long and 37 centimetres wide!

Beefsteak fungus

Shaggy ink cap

Slugs find fungi very tasty.

Three different kinds of bracket fungi

Not all the large fungi are white in colour. The shaggy ink cap is black and white. Fly agaric is red, and bracket fungus is brown. Mould on bread is green, and mould found on tomatoes is often black. In fact fungi can be almost any colour: mauve, orange, yellow or even blue!

If you collect mushrooms from the fields, you must be very careful. Field or horse mushrooms, those most generally eaten, are quite large. You may find blue caps in late summer and early autumn, and these too are edible. But some fungi growing wild can be extremely poisonous and can even cause death!

In the British Isles, the only mushrooms sold in the shops are usually specially grown. They are grown in caves or sheds which are kept at the same temperature all the time so that crops can be gathered all through the year.

People are not the only ones to enjoy fungi and grow them specially. Parasol ants have been growing one particular kind of fungus for millions of years. They have special toadstool gardens deep in their nests, and they eat the hyphae (roots) which they grow.

Termites, which are also called white ants, are found in Australia and Africa. They live in large mounds called termitaria, and they too grow a fungus and eat it.

Donna's Day Out

Donna was pleased with her brother Willoughby when he won a trip to the zoo for their class. She had been before, and she liked the children's part of the zoo best.

This time she went there first, and stood watching with Mrs Evans the teacher as a boy fed the lambs from a bucket with holes and tubes in it. The lambs didn't take long to empty it!

While they were standing there, Mrs Evans suddenly said, "What's that?" And turned round to discover that a goat was trying to eat her coat! She looked very cross for a moment, then she began to laugh.

The boy with the lambs grinned too and said, "Those goats will eat anything!" Then he said to Donna, "Some people keep goats at home for milk, you know. It's supposed to be easier to digest for babies and for people who're ill. That's because the fat globules in it are much smaller than those in cow's milk."

Donna looked at the goat again, but decided she'd stick to cow's milk. She wandered off by herself towards the kangaroos. She had passed them once, but the animals had been at the other end of the paddock and she couldn't see them properly. Now one of them was halfway down the field, moving nearer and nearer to the fence as it ate the grass. While she waited patiently for it to come closer, Donna read a little notice at one side of the fence.

It said that kangaroos are marsupials, which means "pouched mammals" (from the word *marsupium* which means pouch) and that all the pouched mammals in the world are native to Australia and New Zealand, except the opossums of America.

The kangaroo has a pouch in which it carries its baby. The baby is called a joey. It stays in the pouch for 8 months.

The koala's favourite food is eucalyptus leaves.

There are many different kinds of kangaroos from the great red kangaroo which is as tall as a man, down to the rat kangaroo and wallabies which may be as little as 30 centimetres high.

Donna was very surprised to read that the koala is a marsupial, and eats only one kind of food – the leaves and shoots of the eucalyptus tree. She had always thought the koala was a bear. She liked the sound of the flying phalanger, which is a marsupial a bit like a squirrel that can glide through the air. The notice mentioned other strange animals from Australia, like the duckbilled platypus, which is a mammal that lays eggs.

Then there were a few sentences about the actual pouch itself, where marsupials keep their babies until they're old enough to look after themselves. Even when the babies are quite big, they will still jump into their mother's pouch when danger is near! The pouch is like a big elastic bag, lined with fur. When a baby kangaroo is born, it is only about $2\frac{1}{2}$ centimetres long. Its mother licks a pathway through her fur to make it easy for the baby to crawl into her pouch. Then the baby fastens on to her teat to drink milk and grow.

At one time in the world's past, there were marsupials in many parts of the world, even in

Europe. At that time, the continent of Australia was still joined to South Africa and India. Then slowly, over millions of years, it drifted apart, and was cut off by the sea. In most other parts of the world, marsupials died out, but in Australia they went on developing as a separate group of animals.

Donna had been so interested in what she was reading that she'd forgotten all about the kangaroos nearby for the moment.

A slight movement caught the edge of her eye, and she looked away from the notice to see a kangaroo on the other side of the fence, about three metres away. It had its head up, looking at her – and there was a baby kangaroo looking at her as well, from the pouch!

Donna couldn't believe her luck. She started to talk in a quiet voice to the kangaroo, much as she would have talked to her puppy at home. "Come on, then," she said softly. "Come and show me your beautiful baby." The kangaroo looked back at her steadily – and hopped towards her.

"Come on, then," said Donna again. "That really is a beautiful baby." The kangaroo came so close that Donna could have touched it if the fence hadn't been there.

"It's really a bit like a sheep or a deer," thought Donna. "And it eats grass like one."

Suddenly someone shouted "Donna." She turned round to see her friend Jean waving to her. They were going to see the reptile house.

When Donna turned back to the kangaroo to say goodbye, it had gone. It was halfway up the field again. It stood still and upright for a moment longer, then bent its head to graze.

This opossum comes from Brazil.

Horses

Shire horses working

Przewalski's wild horse

Onager

People and horses have been together for thousands of years. The horse has been used for sheer hard work and also for pleasure, in such sports as show jumping and racing.

At one time, horses pulling a plough were a familiar sight on farms in Britain. Then the tractor came along, and fewer and fewer plough horses were to be seen.

If soil is heavy, however, it can be damaged by a tractor. And in fenland, tractors can easily get bogged down in wet fields. So in such places the horse is still used, because it can do the job so much better than a tractor could.

Some of the most famous breeds of horses were developed for working on farms. The largest horse in the world is the Shire horse, which is usually about 18 hands high. The height of a horse is measured in "hands", and a hand is 10 centimetres (4 inches). So a Shire horse is nearly 2 metres high at the withers (the highest point of a horse's back, at the base of its neck).

Shire horses are descended from the battle chargers of the Middle Ages. In those days, both rider and horse wore heavy armour, so that the horse had to be big and strong. The three other breeds seen most often on British farms are the Clydesdale, the Suffolk Punch, and the Percheron which came originally from northern France.

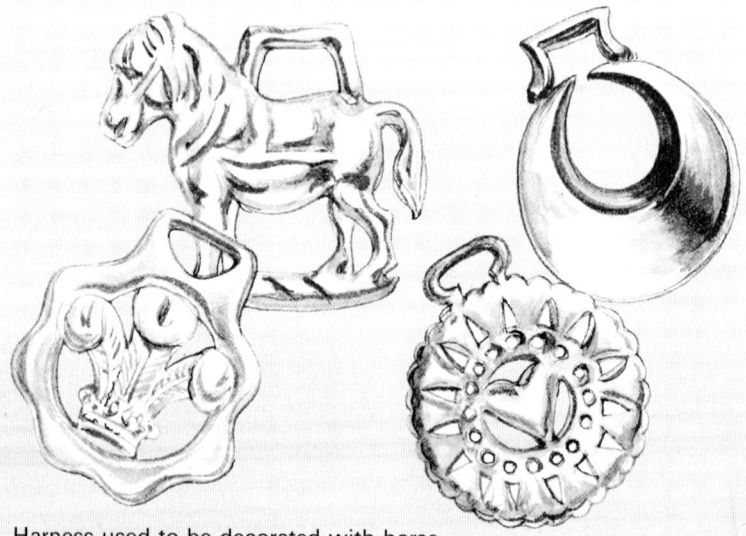

Harness used to be decorated with horse brasses like these to protect the horse from evil spirits and sickness.

Horses haven't always been farm animals. Long ago, they were hunted for food. Then they began to be ridden. Later on they were used to pull carts and coaches. Because of their many uses, they were always considered valuable, and always carefully looked after. The horse brasses which today are used to decorate harness were put there at one time to protect the horse from evil spirits, sickness and harm of any kind.

Nowadays racehorses, which can run at 56 kilometres an hour, are the most valuable animals anywhere in the world. In 1980, a racehorse was valued at over fourteen million pounds! Incidentally, all the top racehorses bred in Britain can trace their ancestry back to just three Arab stallions which were brought to Britain in the eighteenth century.

Nearly all horses are tame, but there is one truly wild horse that lives in Mongolia. It has the strange name of Przewalski's wild horse, after the Russian explorer Nicholas Przewalski who discovered it. Unfortunately this wild horse is still hunted for its meat, in spite of laws which have been passed to protect it. So it may become extinct.

Included in the horse family are also zebras and asses. There are three main kinds of zebra, and they all live in Africa. One of them, Grevy's zebra, stands as tall as a horse. It grazes on the plains of northern Kenya, Ethiopia and Somalia. Up to a hundred years ago, there was a fourth kind of zebra called a quagga. But it was hunted so much that it became extinct.

Of the three species of wild asses, two live in Asia and one lives in Africa. The Asiatic kinds are the onager and the kiang, and the African kind is the Nubian wild ass. Each of the three can run as fast as a deer, and all of them are hunted for their meat.

When a male ass and a female horse breed, they produce an animal called a mule. When a female ass and a male horse breed, they produce an animal called a hinny. To produce a hinny or a mule, the parents always have to be an ass and a horse. Hinnies and mules are themselves unable to breed. Mules are just as strong as horses, but are more sure-footed. Because of this they are used to carry things in mountainous places. They are very hardy animals.

The Great Spotted Woodpecker

If you hear a sharp drumming sound when you are walking through a wood, it is likely to be a woodpecker. It makes a noise just like a loud rattle as it pecks a hole in a tree or a piece of dead wood. Most birds sing to tell other birds about their territory, but the woodpecker makes its drumming sound to drive away rivals.

With their chisel-like beaks and powerful neck muscles, woodpeckers dig into trees in search of sap and wood-boring insects, which they lick out with their long sticky tongues. The green woodpecker can stretch its tongue as much as 15 centimetres beyond the end of its beak to hunt out insects hiding under the bark of a tree.

All over the world there are many different kinds of woodpeckers, and they are all handsome creatures. In Great Britain there are three kinds. There is the biggest one, the green woodpecker and there are also the lesser spotted woodpecker, and the great spotted woodpecker.

Great spotted woodpeckers are not only found in Great Britain. They are also found right across Europe and Central Asia and as far away as China and Japan. They can be seen in deciduous forests and in coniferous forests, and for the past few years they have even been coming into gardens to visit bird tables.

A hundred years ago, great spotted woodpeckers disappeared completely from Scotland. No one knows why they did so, and now they have returned once more.

The great spotted woodpecker is about 23 centimetres long. The cock and the hen are very alike – black and white with a red patch under their tails. The cock however also has a band of red across his head. On young birds, the whole crown is red.

To make a nest, the cock and the hen peck a hole in a tree, usually about 3 metres from the ground. They don't line the nest in any way, except for a few chips of wood.

In May, the hen lays about half a dozen white eggs, which hatch sixteen days later. Then for three weeks, both parents feed the nestlings until they are able to fly away and look after themselves.

Parrots

Parrots have always been popular with people. They are affectionate birds and enjoy company. If you keep a parrot as a pet, you must talk to it and take an interest in it. Otherwise it will be very unhappy.

Parrots are also intelligent. Some are good at imitating human voices, and can even learn tricks.

The two parrots that most people know best are the African grey parrot and the Amazon parrot. The African grey parrot is grey with a squared-off red tail. It lives in the rain forests of Africa, and it is the best talker of the parrot family. A male African grey parrot won the title of "Best talking parrot-like bird" for twelve years running, at the yearly Cage and Aviary Bird Show held in London. He could speak nearly a thousand words, and when he stopped entering the show in 1977 he had never been beaten!

Amazon parrots live in rain forests as well, but on the other side of the Atlantic Ocean. They are found from Mexico to the north of South America. They are also very good talkers, but they are much more brightly coloured than the African grey parrot. Their plumage is mostly grass green and yellow, with added patterns of blue, red and black.

These two kinds are by no means the only kinds of parrots in the world however. There are over 300 species altogether. Some are as small as 8 centimetres long (smaller than a canary) and others can be as much as 100 centimetres long.

A parrot's beak is hooked to help the bird to deal with the sort of food it prefers. A parrot's toes help it to climb trees.

It's easy to recognise members of the parrot family. They all have hooked bills, rounded wings and short legs. Their feet are different as well – they have two toes facing forwards and two pointing backwards, to help them to climb trees. Woodpeckers and cuckoos have feet like this too, but most birds have three toes pointing forwards and one pointing backwards.

Most of the parrot family are found in the tropical parts of the world where there is always fruit and nuts for them to eat. All those that are found in Britain and the cooler parts of the world have been taken there or bred in captivity. Parrots could never exist in the wild in Britain because during the winter there would be no food available for them.

Macaw eggs and chicks

Nearly all parrots nest in holes in trees. Some lay their eggs on the bare floor of the hole, others put in leaves or bark strips to add some softness. Parrot eggs are white, and the larger species usually lay only two, once a year. Smaller species may lay as many as eight or even nine eggs, two or three times a year. Parrots look after their young for several weeks after they hatch – much longer than most birds do.

African grey parrot

Male and female eclectus parrots. Which is the male?

Rainbow lorikeet feeding on an umbrella tree

Palm cockatoo

Scarlet macaw

Blue-fronted Amazon parrot

The monk parakeet of South America builds a large stick nest in a tree. Unusually, a number of these birds live in it together as a community.

The tiny pygmy parrot of New Guinea and nearby islands hollows out its nest in a termitarium (the home of a termite colony). Pygmy parrots are birds of the forest and unlike other parrots they have weak bills. This may be the reason that they eat a food that no other birds touch – fungi.

Some kinds of parrots nest in cracks in rock or in earthen caves. The night parrot from Australia, and the kea and the owl parrot, both of New Zealand, all do this. The owl parrot is very unusual because it can't fly at all. It feeds on roots.

The ground parrot of southern Australia and Tasmania makes its nest in a leaf-lined shallow bowl shape under a bush. At one time the ground parrot was hunted with dogs, because it runs in the grass and rises from the ground like a quail.

People often keep budgerigars as pets. They are small parrots which come from the grasslands of Australia, where they live in large flocks of ten or twenty thousand birds. In very dry weather, the flocks of birds may fly great distances in search of food and water. Wild budgerigars are about 14 centimetres long, and have bright yellow heads with blue and black stripes across the cheeks. Their underparts are green and their backs are yellow with closely spaced brown bars across them.

Nowadays careful breeding has produced pet budgerigars that are one colour all over. They can be yellow, green, blue, white, and even lilac and cream.

In the United States of America, budgerigars are called parakeets. The name parakeet however is also used for many other small and medium-sized parrots that are found in India, Malaya, Africa and South America. One of the most beautiful parakeets is the Alexandrine parakeet. Its head has bands of red, black, purple and turquoise, its wings and body are bright green, and on each shoulder there is a red patch. Its long tail is sky blue.

Cockatoos are medium-sized parrots, mostly with short tails. Their plumage may be grey, black, pink, or white, sometimes tinged with pink or yellow.

In the rain forests of Australia and New Guinea there are palm cockatoos which are black all over except for the cheeks which are red. They have long fine black crests.

Another black cockatoo is the red-tailed cockatoo. He has a black beak and his tail has a red band on it. The female however is brownish black with yellow spots, and narrow bars of yellow and orange on her underparts. Her black tail also has bars of yellow and orange on it, and she has a white beak. The red-tailed cockatoo lives in all kinds of places in Australia – in dense forests, coastal woodland, and grasslands.

In the parrot family, there are usually only small differences between male and female birds. In one species however – the eclectus parrot of the tropical rain forest of Australia – the male is green and the female is dark red. For this reason they were thought for many years to be two separate species!

Australia and New Zealand have yet other kinds of parrots – the loris and the lorikeets. These are parrots with special brush-like tongues which they use to feed on nectar from the blossom of flowering trees and shrubs.

Flock of wild budgies in Australia

Purple crowned lorikeet

A pair of African lovebirds

Ground parrot

Alexandrine parakeet

Macaws live in the tropical rain forests of Central and South America, and they are the largest members of the parrot family. They are called macaws because they eat the violet-perfumed oil nuts of the macaw palm tree. They have enormous beaks which they use to crack these very hard nuts and also to grip branches as they climb about in the trees.

South American Indians living in the rain forests use macaw feathers to decorate their head dresses and clothes. This is because the birds have very bright glossy green, blue, yellow and red plumage.

There aren't many species of parrot found in Africa, but some of the most attractive of all live there. They are the small short-tailed parrots called love birds. These little green birds are called love birds because a pair will sit close together for long periods, preening each other's feathers and showing affection in other ways.

Members of the parrot family are very long-lived. When a greater sulphur-crested cockatoo called Cocky died in London Zoo in 1982, he had been there for 57 years – and he was probably at least 40 years old when he first went to the zoo in 1925. And a red and green Amazon parrot said to have been hatched in captivity in 1870 did not die until 1975 – he was just over 104 years old!

Snakes

Of all the animals on Earth, snakes are probably the ones that people hate and fear most. It may be because of the strange way snakes move, or it may be because of their shape. It may be because people know that some snakes can be very dangerous indeed.

Snakes are reptiles, and they belong to the same group of creatures as turtles, crocodiles and lizards. They stare without blinking, because they have no eyelids. They have no legs, although some pythons and boa constrictors do have hind limbs hidden inside their bodies.

There are over 3000 different species of snakes, and they are found in nearly every part of the world. The greatest number of snakes however live in the tropics where it is warmer. It is only in these tropical parts of the world that the really large snakes are to be found.

Snakes can't be active unless they're warm. A snake's body temperature depends on its surroundings, because a snake can't control its temperature from within as mammals do. It will bask in warm sunshine, but when the direct rays of the sun become too hot, it will shield itself by sheltering in a hole or a cave.

When it is cold, snakes can't move quickly. In the colder parts of the world, they hibernate during the winter. They don't emerge until the warmer days of spring.

One snake that does this is the adder which lives in northern Europe, ranging as far north as the Arctic Circle. It is the only poisonous snake to be found in Britain. Adders are not dangerous if they are left alone. Many people have been bitten because they accidentally trod on an adder when it was basking in the sunlight. Ten people have died in the last hundred years after being bitten by an adder. The most recent was in 1975.

There are only two other snakes to be found in Great Britain. They are the grass snake and the smooth snake. Neither of them is dangerous, but if they are picked up they may squirt out an evil smelling liquid.

Adder

Grass snake

This smooth snake is eating a lizard.

Smooth snakes, found only in the south of England, can vary greatly in colour. They may be grey, or brown, or even red, with dark spots down their backs and a dark patch on the sides and tops of their heads. Not surprisingly, they have smooth scales, unlike the adder and the grass snake.

The smooth snake eats mostly young lizards, slow worms, small mammals, insects and nestlings. The snake can't poison its prey, so it grips it with its jaws, then coils round it until it stops struggling.

Both the adder and the smooth snake are about half a metre long. The female adder is usually about ten centimetres longer than the male.

The grass snake is the longest of the three British snakes. The female may be as long as 90 centimetres – 30 centimetres longer than the male. The grass snake is easily recognised because it has two yellowish or orange crescent-shaped patches behind its head. Sometimes these look almost like a ring round the creature's neck, giving it its other name of ringed snake.

The female grass snake lays her eggs in June or July, and they take about six to ten weeks to hatch. The baby snakes are about 18 centimetres long, and they bite their way through the leathery egg shells with a special egg tooth that disappears as they grow older. Grass snakes are usually found close to streams, ditches and ponds. They are very good swimmers, and hunt newts, frogs, toads and fish, which they swallow alive.

Snakes have strangely-hinged jaws which enable them to swallow quite large creatures that may be seen as a lump inside the body of the snake for some time after the prey has been eaten.

Snakes' teeth are thin and curve backwards, so they are no use for chewing. Using these teeth, the snake grips its prey, then by moving its lower jaw backwards and forwards, it gradually draws the victim into its mouth and down its throat. Its powerful throat muscles force the prey into the snake's stomach, where it is slowly digested. This can take a long time, and has some disadvantages. While it is swallowing its prey, for example, the snake may be attacked. Then, if it has swallowed a very large victim, it will not be able to move very quickly for some time afterwards. So again, if it is attacked, there is little it can do. If this happens, the grass snake will pretend to be dead to protect itself.

There is one advantage, however. Once a snake has eaten a large meal, it may not have to go hunting for several months afterwards.

In Britain a creature that is often mistaken for a

Slow worm

snake is a slow worm. Sometimes it is called a blind worm, although it is neither blind nor a worm. It is a smooth-scaled limbless lizard with eyelids, and it can grow to about half a metre long. Its body is covered in small tight-fitting scales which may be either grey or a deep bronze colour. The young have a dark strip down their backs, and this is often seen in females too. Slow worms, like other lizards, feed mainly on earthworms, slugs and snails. Like other lizards, they also can shed their tails in order to escape if they are seized by another animal, and later grow a new one. Snakes cannot do this. On the other hand, like snakes but not like other lizards, slow worms shed their skins in one piece.

Strange as it may seem, no snakes or even slow worms are to be found in one part of the British Isles – Ireland. The patron saint of Ireland, St Patrick, is said to have driven all the snakes away. Apart from the cold polar regions, there are only two other places where snakes are not to be found – New Zealand and Hawaii.

The king cobra is one of the most dangerous members of the snake family.

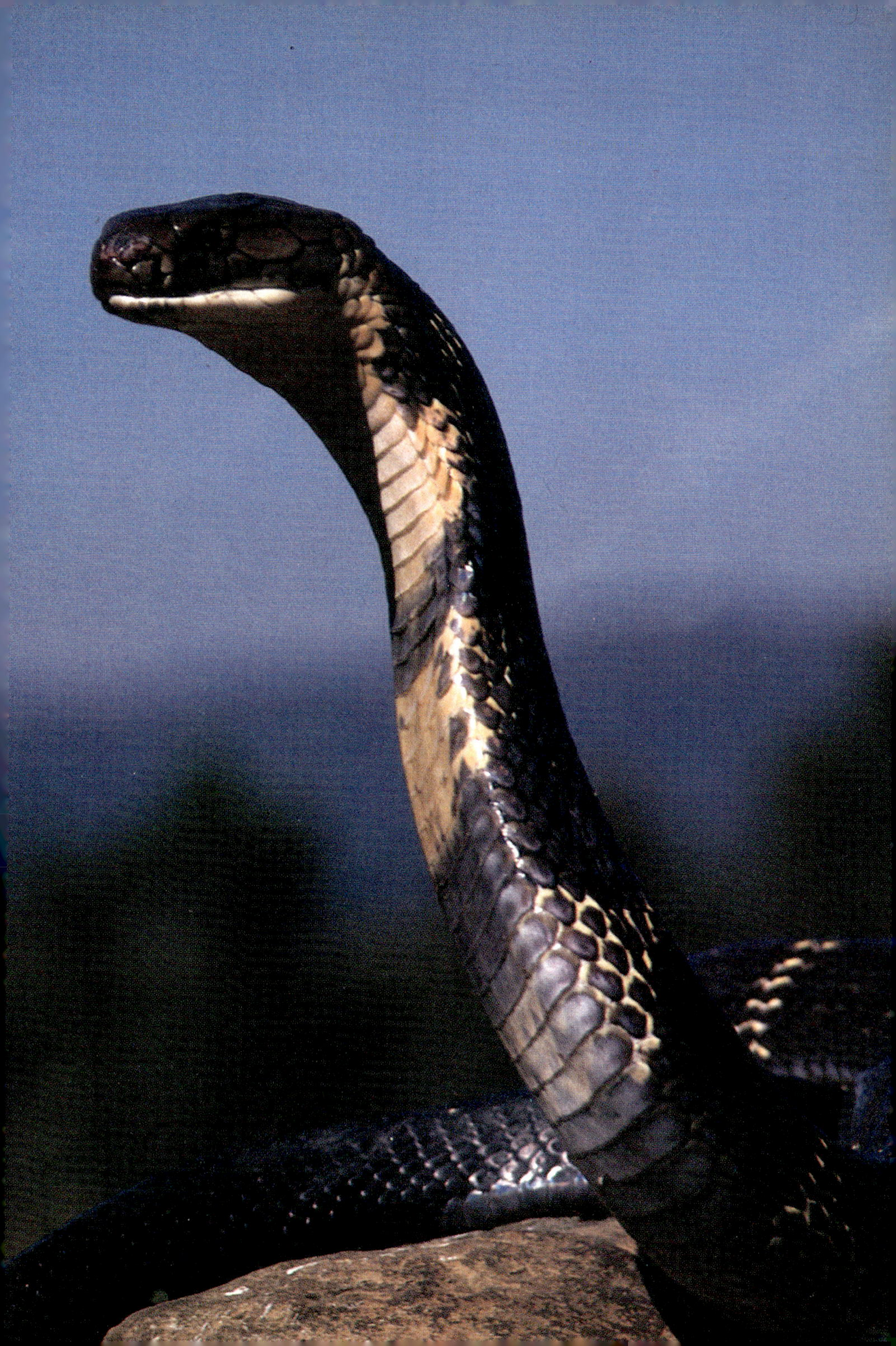

Three ways in which snakes move

Zigzag
The snake darts its head and neck forward, grips the ground with its neck and pulls up the rest of its body quickly in a V shape.

Moving in a straight line
The snake wriggles along slowly by gripping the ground with the scales on the underside of its body and pusing itself forward.

Sidewinding
The snake moves by gripping the ground with its head and tail and throwing the middle of its body sideways. This kind of movement leaves parallel tracks on the sandy ground.

Snakes can move in several different ways. When moving slowly in a straight line, they grip the ground or the surface of a tree with the wide scales on the underside of their bodies. These are moved forward and pushed backwards in such a way that the snake seems to flow along by rippling its muscles. When a snake wants to move quickly, it may use one of two other methods. Many snakes can move very quickly in a zigzag motion along the ground, folding their bodies into a series of loops along the ground before thrusting their heads forward.

Sidewinding is another way. The snake moves sideways by gripping the ground with its neck and tail, then throwing the middle of its body forward. Then it moves its head and tail in the same direction.

All snakes shed their skins several times a year, and some have been known to do this as much as a dozen times. Even the eye covering comes off with the skin. The scales of a snake are not separate, like those of a fish. The shape of each scale is formed by folds in the snake's body.

Before a snake sheds its skin, it grows a new one underneath. When it is time for the skin to come off, its colour becomes dull. The snake rubs its head against a hard surface until the skin begins to come off. Then once it has freed the skin round its head, it wriggles free, leaving the old skin all in one piece, but inside out. The old skin is colourless and transparent. That's because the snake's body is the coloured part, and its skin is only a very thin covering, made of a material something like your fingernails. Although snakes often have a shiny skin, it is dry and not unpleasant to touch.

Snakes are very quiet creatures, and they cannot hear sounds because they have no ears. A snake won't go away if you shout at it – but it will if you stamp your foot at it, because it can feel the vibrations.

Brazilian
boa constrictor

More than 400 of the snake species in the world are poisonous, but only about half of those can be harmful to people.

The most dangerous are perhaps the members of the cobra family. When frightened or alarmed, a cobra will rear up and spread out its hood. (The hood is formed by long ribs inside soft folds of skin attached to the side of the snake's neck.) If this action does not frighten off its enemy, the cobra will threaten to bite. The African spitting cobra is especially dangerous, for the venom from its fangs can cause blindness if it enters its enemy's eyes.

If the cobra is forced to strike, it will hang on to its victim, forcing venom into it and taking all its power away.

Cobras are found in Africa, India and south-east Asia. The largest when fully grown will measure up

Banded krait

Coral snake

Anaconda

Green mamba hatching

Python digesting a deer

to 3 metres long. Some cobras are black, others are pink or brown, and many have strange and beautiful markings. If disturbed by people, cobras will usually try to escape. If one is cornered, however, it can prove a deadly enemy.

One of the most dangerous snakes in India is the krait. It is not very big, and many people in India always shake their shoes before putting them on, in case one of these snakes has slipped inside.

The most poisonous of all the poisonous snakes in the world is a sea snake which lives off the coast of North West Australia. Most snakes are solitary, but sea snakes are known to travel sometimes in large groups. Although they are so poisonous, they hardly ever bite anyone. They are timid, and don't attack people who are swimming or diving. All sea snakes must come to the surface to breathe, but they can stay underwater for long periods. They are good swimmers – some can even swim backwards.

The most poisonous land snake is the small-scaled or fierce snake, which lives in Queensland, Australia.

Pythons and boa constrictors are not poisonous. These snakes kill their prey by coiling round it. They are also the largest snakes.

The reticulated python which is found in south-east Asia, Indonesia and the Philippines, is the longest snake in the world. It usually reaches a length of 6 metres and more, and one has been recorded of 10 metres. The anaconda, which lives in the marshes and slow-moving rivers of South America, can grow to about the same length, but it is a much heavier creature. A female anaconda killed in Brazil in 1960 was 8.45 metres long and measured 111 centimetres round its body. It is believed to have weighed over 200 kilograms.

There is an amazing variety of snakes. Some, like the yellow, black and red coral snake, use their bright colours to frighten away their enemies. Others hiss in a threatening manner. The rattlesnake makes a warning sound by shaking the end of its tail.

Some snakes are tiny. The Syrian thread snake is little bigger than a pencil.

The Asian flying snake can do something very unusual – it can flatten the underside of its body and glide to the ground from the top of a tree.

One of the things to be said for snakes is that in Great Britain and many other parts of the world, they help to keep down the number of rats and mice.

Against that must be set the fact that in the tropical parts of the world, between thirty and forty thousand people are known to die from snake bite each year.

The End of a Perfect Day

Donna's best friend at school was a girl called Fiona. She had red hair and she came from Scotland. When Willoughby won the story prize for their class, Fiona was just as pleased as Donna was. She loved going to the zoo.

All the children had their own favourites, and Fiona liked the apes and monkeys best. There are lots and lots of different kinds, but they all seem to have bright intelligent eyes and almost human faces. Fiona knew that was because they are distant relations of people – they are primates or top animals.

There are four kinds of great apes. Gorillas, which are the biggest, can be 1.8 metres tall and weigh 270 kilograms. Chimpanzees are the cleverest, and can be taught to do some of the things that people do.

Chimpanzees are our closest relative in the animal world.

Orang utans are very rare and live only in the islands of Sumatra and Borneo in Indonesia. Gibbons, which are the smallest, have very long arms.

Fiona liked the chimpanzees best of all. She liked the noisy way they always seemed to show off when people were watching them. It was as if they were really enjoying themselves. Chimpanzees are from the tropical forests of Africa, where they live on fruit and berries. They also eat termites, and may even kill and eat monkeys and other animals. As many as twenty may live together in a group.

Chimpanzees are our closest relative. Their brains are about a third the size of our brains, but they can learn to do all sorts of things. They can use simple tools, and they use sticks as weapons.

There are only two main groups of monkeys – New World ones from South America, and Old World ones from Asia and Africa. Altogether there are about 150 different kinds.

As Fiona walked through the monkey house, she saw some capuchin monkeys from South America – and one of them was very tiny indeed. It was jet black, with a white face, chest and shoulders, and its bright eyes twinkled at her through the wire. She saw from the notice that it was a white-throated capuchin monkey. In South America these monkeys usually travel in troops of twelve to forty, sometimes going through the trees in single file. The notice also said that this sort of monkey was nearly as intelligent as a chimpanzee, and was well-known because organ-grinders used to keep them many years ago.

Fiona put her hand near the wire, and the little monkey put its paw through to touch her.

Mrs Evans walked past at that moment. "Don't go so near the wire, Fiona," she said. "You might get bitten."

Fiona drew her hand back, then looked at the little monkey again. It was pulling at a broken piece of wire, making the hole bigger. Fiona leaned forward and bent the sharp piece of wire back and then – afterwards she could never remember how it happened – the monkey was out, sitting on her sleeve.

Fiona looked round guiltily, but no one was watching, and Mrs Evans had gone. She opened her anorak. The little monkey seemed to know what to do. It sat just above the waistband of her anorak. She tightened the cord, then pulled the zip up again.

She looked round again, but no one had noticed.

Soon it was time to go home. The teacher, Mrs Evans, counted them on to the bus, and the door slid shut.

The children were very quiet as the bus drove along. It had been a super day, and they were all tired. One or two, including Fiona, went to sleep. Mrs Evans was tired too. She sat back in her seat and closed her eyes.

The bus stopped suddenly with a jerk, and everyone woke up. The driver was staring up into the mirror from which he could see everyone in the bus. He looked as if he couldn't believe his eyes.

He was staring at Fiona. Mrs Evans turned to see what was wrong.

And there was the monkey, its little face poking out of the top of Fiona's anorak.

Everyone began to talk at once, and there was the most tremendous fuss. The bus turned round, and they went back to the zoo.

Capuchin monkey

Fiona cuddled the little monkey all the way back, and its head was wet with her tears when she had to hand it over. It tried to cling to her. It didn't want to go back either.

"It really is better off with its mother, you know, Fiona," said Mrs Evans gently. "It would have been unhappy away from the other monkeys."

Fiona gulped and wiped her eyes. Then as the bus went on its way, she began to dream. When she grew up, she was going to work in a zoo....

Insects

Insects are found in every part of the world, wherever there is plant life or animals on which they can feed. Over three-quarters of all the species of creatures in the world are insects. They are found in the cold north of the Arctic, in the cold south of the Antarctic, and in all the places in between – in deserts, lakes, rivers, grassy meadows, on mountain tops and on animals everywhere. Some – though not many – are found in the sea.

Wasp nest

Ladybird eating an aphid

Grasshopper

There are insects of all colours, shapes and sizes. Over eight hundred thousand different kinds are known. In Great Britain alone there are over twenty thousand different species of insects.

On one single square metre of moist soil, over fifteen hundred different insects may be found. So that on a hectare of ground, there could be as many as fifteen *million* insects!

Some are so small that it is almost impossible to see them. Others can be very large. One of the biggest is the African giant swallow-tailed butterfly. It has a wingspan of almost a quarter of a metre. The giant stick insect has a body which is 330 millimetres long. When its legs are stretched out in front of its body, its total length is over half a metre!

The name "insect" comes from a Latin word which means "cut in". All insects have three parts, and some of them really look as if they have almost been cut into three pieces. Those pieces are the head, the thorax (the chest) and the stomach, known as the abdomen. On a wasp or a butterfly, the head, thorax and abdomen are easy to see, but it is more difficult to see these three parts on, say, a ladybird.

Insects have interesting heads. Sticking out can be seen the antennae or feelers which are used for smelling. These antennae are very sensitive. Some male moths are able to smell a female from a distance of almost two kilometres. (Flies can detect sweet things just by walking on them!)

Antennae are used for touching. Bees pass messages to each other by touching antennae.

On the sides of an insect's head are its large eyes. These are not ordinary eyes – they are compound eyes and they give the insect a very wide view.

Insects have different ways of feeding. Some have jaws that they use to chew, moving them from side to side. Other insects can only suck their food. The greenfly has a long thin beak which it pushes into plants so that it can suck up the sap.

Fleas feed on warmblooded animals. Like greenfly, they have a needle-like beak with which they pierce the skin before sucking up blood. When the animal on which they are living dies, the fleas leave it to find another live animal to feed on.

Ants and earwigs chew their food with their strong jaws. Houseflies use their long tongues to suck up liquid into their mouths. Butterflies have a long tube, like a straw, with which they suck up nectar from flowers. This tube is called a proboscis. When it is not being used, it is coiled up beneath the butterfly's head.

An adult insect always has six legs, which are attached to the thorax. If it has wings, they too are attached to its thorax. Although this part of the insect looks like its chest, insects do not have lungs, nor do they breathe through their mouths. The very smallest insects breathe through their skins, but most insects breathe through tiny holes in the sides of their bodies.

Insects don't have backbones. They don't even have skeletons. Instead they have a tough shell-like skin which has joints in it, something like a suit of armour. This shell protects the insect's simple heart, kidneys and stomach, which are inside the abdomen.

Woodlouse eggs hatching

Adult woodlouse

Wood ant nest

A colony of wood ants

An insect's eye is made up of thousands of separate little lenses. This is a magnified picture of the eye of a fruit fly.

A few insects, like the bristle tail and the silver fish, look the same from the moment they hatch to the moment they die. They just grow bigger by casting off their skins. The outer skin of an insect can't grow bigger, so when the creature grows so big that its skin is too tight, it casts off the old skin. Underneath it has a new skin which stretches while it is still soft.

Some insects *do* alter their shapes slightly each time they cast off their skins. Grasshoppers and crickets do this. When they are young, they do not have any wings, but after they have cast off their skins two or three times, wings can be seen.

Insects that live in colonies and look after one another, each one having its own particular job, are called social insects. Ants, termites, bees and wasps are amongst them. They build homes for themselves and look after their young. Some, like the parasol ant and the termite, are even farmers, and grow their own crops of fungi to eat.

Most people think that all insects are harmful. Mosquitos carry the diseases of yellow fever and malaria, and the African tsetse fly spreads sleeping sickness. Even lice can carry typhus.

Houseflies and bluebottles can ruin food, and others such as greenfly and locusts can destroy a farmer's crops. A great many such as midges, bed bugs and wasps can be nuisances.

But many insects are helpful to people. Without them, flowers and plants would not be pollinated. Most of this work is done by bees as they search for nectar, which they make into honey. A few insects such as ladybirds help gardeners, by hunting greenfly and blackfly.

We unwind silk from the chrysalis of the silkworm moth, and we obtain dyes and drugs from other insects.

Lastly, insects are important as food for birds and small animals.

Bats

In China and other countries of the East, bats are used in pictures to mean happiness and contentment. In the West, they are used to mean horror, and are thought of as secretive and mysterious.

One reason for this may be that very few people have ever seen these animals clearly. In Britain and the cooler parts of the world, bats hide in buildings, caves and tree hollows. Hardly any of the species of bats are ever seen flying in daylight. Nearly all of them spend the day hanging by their hind feet, upside down, with their wings folded round them. So the only time they can usually be seen is when they come out to feed at night.

Bats are mammals that can fly. You may have heard of animals called flying squirrels, but they can't really fly. They can only glide through the air with the help of flaps of skin that stretch between their fore and hind legs. Bats however can fly just as well as birds, and they are the *only* mammals that can do so.

The scientific name for the family of bats is *Chiroptera*. This is a Greek word meaning "hand-wing" – and that's just what the wings of a bat look like. They have long arms and extremely long fingers covered with skin stretching from the sides of the body to the hind feet and the tail.

Most bats have very poor eyesight, but they can catch insects and other prey in complete darkness, even avoiding obstacles as small as thin wires that may be in their way. They do this in the same way as some other mammals such as whales and dolphins. They send out a sound which is bounced back to them as an echo by the object which is in their way, showing them where it is. The clicking sound which bats send out for this purpose is too high pitched for humans to hear.

There are about 900 different species of bats. That's an amazing number, because there are only about 4000 species of mammals altogether on the Earth!

Bats can be divided into two main groups: bats that eat fruit, and bats that eat insects.

Fruit eating bats include the biggest bats of all, the "flying foxes", which are not however related to foxes at all. They are called that because of their fox-like heads. One, the Malay flying fox, measures one and a half metres from wing tip to wing tip. Its body on the other hand may be only about 30 or 40 centimetres long.

A colony of greater horseshoe bats in hibernation

Bechstein's bat

Fruit bats all have very large eyes and can see well at night, although they cannot see in total darkness. They have large blunt teeth.

There are no fruit eating bats in Britain. They are only found in the warmer parts of the world, because they must be able to find fruit all through the year.

The wingspan of the very largest insect eating bat is only three-quarters of a metre, and these bats are in general smaller than fruit eating bats.

Insect eating bats are found in all parts of the world except in deserts and in the very coldest parts. During the summer there is always a plentiful supply of food. Then during the autumn, they eat enormous amounts of insects and become very fat. This is so that in winter, when there are few insects about, the bats can go into the deep sleep we call hibernation.

Many insect eating bats in North America migrate southwards, to spend the winter in a warmer climate where there will be plenty of insects for food. The Mexican free tailed bat is known to fly as much as 1300 kilometres between its winter home in Mexico and its breeding place in the United States.

Insect eating bats have small sharp teeth, but a small group of bats with sharp teeth seek other food. They are the famous vampire bats that live in Central and South America. They feed only on blood.

Vampire bats have two razor sharp front teeth with which they pierce the skin of a sleeping animal. Then they lick the blood. The victim doesn't lose a great deal of blood, and the bite doesn't hurt it. Many of the bats however are already infected with a deadly disease called rabies, and they often pass the disease on to the cattle, horses and dogs which they bite.

A few kinds of tropical bats only feed on nectar, helping to pollinate the flowers in the same way that bees do.

Among the strangest members of the bat family are some which hunt other animals like lizards, mice and other bats. And in Asia there are two species which catch fish by trailing their claws in the sea as they fly over the water. There is a fishing bat in Central America which uses its special radar or echo location to detect fish from the ripples they make on the water!

Although most kinds of bats live in the hotter parts of the world, fourteen different species live in the British Isles. They are ugly to look at, but they are completely harmless. They do not cause damage to crops or livestock, either. They are in fact very useful, because they eat vast numbers of insect pests.

Bats have few natural enemies, but in some parts of Africa and Australia people eat them. They are supposed to taste rather like chicken!

For the first few weeks the baby bat clings to its mother as she flies around.

A colony of fruit bats in Sri Lanka. Their droppings kill all the leaves.